*DISCLAIMER: This information is provided "as is". The author, publishers and marketers of this information disclaim any loss or liability, either directly or indirectly as a consequence of applying the information presented herein, or in regard to the use and application of said information. No guarantee is given, either expressed or implied, in regard to the merchantability, accuracy, or acceptability of the information.*

# 15 Top Ways To Save Money

## Table of Contents

**How to save on insurance**

**How to save on auto loans**

**How to save on mortgage loans**

**How to save on credit cards**

**How to save on gasoline**

**How to save on car repairs**

**How to save on home improvement**

**How to save on home heating and energy**

**How to save on phone service**

**How to save on major appliances**

**How to save on furniture**

**How to save on clothing**

**How to save on groceries**

**How to save on vacations**

**How to save on prescription drugs**

# How to save on insurance

How to save on insurance

As much as possible, if it can be done, you must seize every opportunity for you to save on insurance. Here are some tips you can follow.

Your home insurance:

- If you think about it, you can actually save up to several hundred dollars if you buy insurance from a low-price but licensed insurer. Compare prices of the insurance departments in your state and get the lowest price but most practical company.

- Negotiate a lower selling price with a broker who works for you and not as the mediator to the seller. There may be a conflict of interest if there are too many people involved. So negotiate with just the broker.

Your life insurance:
- If you prefer just insurance protection, and not a savings and investment life policy, you can just buy term life insurance.

- If you would like to purchase whole life insurance, then hold on to one up to 15 years. If you cancel these policies after only two years of having them in your name it will mean double the insurance costs.

- Check the public library about life insurance in your state and get one that suits your personal savings.

## How to save on auto loans

How to Save on Auto Loans

A smart investor knows he must seize every opportunity that comes knocking at his door - as long as it allows him to save more. Auto refinancing is appealing to those whose credit scores are of good history. This is favorable for a buyer who has no negative records on his account whatsoever.

Auto loans gives the buyer the opportunity to refinance their loan at terms that allows them to save their money. However, refinancing is not saving. At least not what most people deem it to be. Refinancing means reducing monthly payments in order to save a little extra money. Car refinance loans are useful in

downsizing.

Auto loans are just a click away, thanks to the Internet. Lenders specializing in refinancing are online to assist possible clients about auto loans. One must submit an application before any negotiation takes place. Provide the same documents required when making a loan at any bank or establishment.

But there are auto loan refinances that do not care even if you have a negative credit history. Refinancing at best rates are available if you have a clear record, but that does not mean that because you were a little off in paying at due time, you will not be able to get the auto loan that you are applying for. You still would but the rate won't be as good as opposed to you having a clear record.

Throughout the duration of the loan, there are opportunities to refinance the car loan. If you are opting for refinancing, know that the options for auto loans are negotiated with the lender beforehand. There can be changes as long as there is the approval from the lender and the person applying for the loan.

If you need refinancing as soon as possible, consult with the lender

and try to work around auto loan refinancing requirements. By updating yourself with the services and programs offered by the various car refinance loan specialists out there, then you are more aware of which one you should choose - depending on the one that works for you best.

Refinance car loan specialists are more than willing to cooperate with

you if the terms you are asking for are favorable for them. The catch

is that when you choose to refinance then the rates are lower and you

will be able to save more. Auto loan refinancing opens more doors to

saving because it reduces your monthly payments at the interest rate of your choice.

Here is a tip before you invest in auto loans, what are your goals for

refinancing? You have to compare with the other auto refinancing

businesses before you fully decide on one. Choose one where you get the best deal and where you will be able to save more. You have a right to do so because it is your money and your investment.

For car owners, investing on auto loans is a wise decision because it gives them better deals. However, before you commit yourself to any refinancing agreement, you have to take into consideration all the terms that are involved in the car financing program you are committing to.

Also, by tapping the equity in your home loan, you will be able to lower the interest payment when buying a car. That is because the home equity loan can actually provide a lower rate as opposed to a car loan. The former is more secured than the latter. You can consult a tax advisor for a second opinion.

If you want you can approach an independent lender before you completely decide on which car to purchase. By arranging the terms and finances before buying the car, dealer financers will be able to assist the consumer in which auto loan refinancing can give him the best deal, making him save the most amount.

You must also be very wary of the zero-interest loans. Just like with any other deals, it may sound tempting but that is not usually the case. You may be buying a car for $18,000 and pay zero interest for two years through the dealer and getting a rebate of $3000, but how sure are you that there is no catch on that offer? If you do take the rebate and finance at the given percent, then who knows you may even save more.

Think twice before you make any decision. Especially since it involves money. Stretch your buck for as long as it would take.

## How to save on mortgage loans

Save on mortgage loans

It is very important to save especially during these tough times. So the best advice anyone can give you is to sign up for the right mortgage loan that is appropriate for your budget.

Mortgage loans are calculated depending on the kind of interest that you signed up for. This is based on the interest rate and the length of mortgage. The shorter the duration of the payment, then the more expensive the bill is on a monthly basis; however, the higher the bill per month, the shorter the time duration of the payment.

It's all about the question of how much you can afford. Create a budget and envision, how much can you actually pay in a month. Think long term. Will you still be earning that particular amount in two, three years time? Do you have enough savings just in case an unforeseen accident occurs? How long can you keep on paying the mortgage?

This is how some lenders calculate how much they can lend you. The housing payment is your total mortgage payment set alongside your monthly income and the total debt ratio – meaning what you are obligated to pay in the big picture.

That's why there's also the question of "Should I buy or rent?" If the person isn't yet financially stable, it is better that he rents in the mean time. However, calculations show that the expenditures on rent are somehow close to signing up for a home mortgage.

Also, there's a great sense of pride in owning your own home. But with that comes the responsibility of paying your bills on time. Plus, now that you're a homeowner, you're also required to set aside a significant amount of your salary for taxes. Owning a home also means paying for utilities such as gas, electricity, water and food.

For you to decide, think whether choosing a home is what's suitable for you at this time. Determine if you have enough to actually afford to buy your own home. If not, then it's better that you rent.

Now here's where the mortgage rates come in. Begin by checking the interest rate and rate movements of a specific mortgage loan you're signing up for. Mortgage rates depend on the Wall Street securities. Keep an eye on the stock market and the mortgage market trends to know the secrets on the direction of where your mortgage is going.

You must also study the APR or the Annual Percentage Rate. By law, mortgage companies are required to disclose the APR to their clients. That is how they should advertise a rate. This is done so that people who signed up under them will be aware of where their rates are going. It represents the real cost of the loan to the borrower and can be seen extensively when the yearly rate is presented. This prevents lenders from hiding fees and for clients to have an open relationship with their mortgage dealers.

As much as possible, try to personally meet with the lender. When money is involved, personal arrangements are better because not only can you clarify better, you could also have an idea of what kind the person is on the end of the phone or at the receiving part of the email you send out.

Now that you have met up with a dealer, know your APR, study the stock market, and then you are ready to lock in your rate. This means that you are ready to commit with a lender and the lender is bound to a promise to this certain interest rate.

From there, you must work on a budget. You must set aside a specific amount from your salary for your mortgage; and, if you can pay faster, then why not? If you have extra money, talk to your lender and ask if you can pay for a higher amount.

For good credit history, always pay more, not less. Pay on time, not late. This is to ensure that you won't have a hard time dealing with insurance matters in the future.

With the right decision-making and the right budget, you won't have any problem with money. It's just having the discipline of creating a budget, sticking to it and paying on time.

If it is arranged as such, notice that you could even save a couple of your dollars.

## How to save on credit cards

How to Save on Credit Cards: The Cost-Effective Ways to Bigger Savings When Times are Tight

Statistical reports prove that Americans are in love with plastic. Consumers know it more as credit cards. In fact, nearly 81% of American households have at least one credit card. They find these plastic as the most convenient tool for shopping and paying utility bills.

The credit cards make payments and expenses so convenient that the average credit card balance Americans have amounts to $8,000. That is, indeed, a great amount of debt.

So if you want to avoid debts and save more on your credit card bills, try to cut back on your expenses and follow the rules on how to save on credit cards.

Here's how:

1. Choose the best credit card

Not all credit cards are created equal. There is a particular credit card that will suit your needs. Getting this type of card will provide you the rewards, services, and interest rates that will suit your needs.

For instance, if you want convenient shopping but can't afford to go the extra mile in shopping expenses, it is best to get a credit card that can offer you with reasonable credit limits. In this way, you will not be tempted to max out your card and accumulate debts you simply can't afford to pay.

2. Go for the lowest interest rate

If you think you can't pay your credit card bills on time but are willing to pay your balances in another period, it is best to get a credit card with lower interest rates.

Consumers may not be aware of this, but one of the reasons why debts are getting higher is based on the interest rates. The actual balances are made worse through interest rate charges.

### 3. Choose the reward credit cards that suits your lifestyle

Don't get a credit card just because it can provide you with several rewards. Not all rewards are worth your time and money.

For instance, a frequent flyer's rewards credit card may not be functional if you aren't a frequent traveler. But if you are, getting a flyer's reward credit card can give you discounts as well as points that can be converted into tickets. This will be savings considering the prices of airline tickets nowadays.

### 4. Keep a record of all your expenses

With credit cards, convenience is the name of the game. However, it doesn't necessarily mean that you neglect your responsibilities. One of which is to keep a record of all your expenses.

In this way, you will be able to identify which purchases weren't necessary at all. So the next time around, you will know what to avoid.

5. Do not keep balances

Never let your balances stay on your credit card bill statements for long. This means that if you have accrued balances for the month, try to pay them immediately.

Paying your minimum balance only won't do you any good. In fact, this might trigger further debts. Besides, interest rates only apply whenever you have balances. And interest rates are additional expenses for you. If you pay your balances monthly, you won't be charged with interest rates, so you get more savings.

6. Be wary of cash advances

If it isn't an emergency, never take cash advances on your credit card. Financial experts say that cash advances reap higher interest rates compared to the ones that you have on your credit card purchases, which are, by nature, soaring as well.

Combination of these two will definitely bring you to debt

problems. Besides, cash advances don't take on certain periods, so that means the charges will take place instantly. That would be very hard if you aren't prepared to pay off your balance immediately.

7. Ask for a lower rate

If you have been an obedient customer and pay your bill on time, it wouldn't hurt you to call your bank or your credit card issuer and ask for a lower rate.

Surveys show that nearly 55% of those who participated in the survey were reported to have trimmed down their interest rates simply by requesting their bank or their credit card companies to act accordingly.

With lower interest rates, you can definitely save more especially if you are the type of credit card holder who doesn't get to pay the balances on time.

All of these things are catered to help you cut back your expenses and save more on your credit cards. These things have been proven effective. It is now up to you if you will heed this advice or not.

Just remember, your actions will always tell you the kind of life you want to live, so better make good choices and start saving now.

## How to save on gasoline

Managing Oil Prices: Tips on How to Save on Gasoline

If you have been spending more than what you can afford on your gasoline consumption, you should trim down the refills. There are many things that are more important than just gasoline, so it goes to show that your money shouldn't revolve on your gasoline bills alone.

Saving on gasoline won't necessarily mean commuting and using your car less often in the same way as not eating food just to save on groceries. That is simply not saving.

Saving on gas would mean maximizing the amount of gasoline you use, thus, giving you better gasoline mileage.

Moreover, with the pries of gasoline nowadays, saving more and maximizing your consumption would definitely give you more than what you have paid for. If you think you can't do away without driving and without using gasoline, you just have to learn how to maximize your gasoline consumption and save more.

Here are a few reminders:

1. A regular tune up on your car can do wonders

A regularly tuned up car will not only mean longer life span of the vehicle but can also guarantee better gas mileage.

You don't have to drive the newest model just to ensure better gas mileage. The performance will entirely depend on how you maintain your car's condition.

If everything is working quite perfectly, you can be sure that you get better gas mileage, which means less gasoline refills.

2. Are you a racer?

If not, then try to drive a little slower. Driving faster than the wind won't only get you into trouble but can also waste a lot of gasoline without you knowing it.

Experts say that "traveling velocity" can put a great impact on your gasoline use. For example, if you drive at 105kph instead of 88kph, you are increasing your gasoline consumption up to 17%. That is a lot of gasoline you have there, and when converted into dollars, that is simply overspending.

3. Be wary of your filter's condition

Filters may seem one of the most neglected parts on a car. Most motorists don't understand the importance of air filters.

Filters make your car's engine more cost-effective. It can create more force and energy and, of course, better gasoline consumption.

If your car has a dirty or congested air filter, replacing them will absolutely perk up your car's gasoline mileage up to 10% more. Besides, having clean air filters all the time will ensure your car engine's optimum performance and durability.

4. Break it more gently

Breaking and accelerating more frequently will not only wear out your car's condition and tires but can also increase you gasoline consumption more than 18%.

So whenever you are on the road, try not to accelerate more than what is recommended. Try to anticipate, as well, the traffic ahead so that you can apply measured, steady brake.

5. Check your tires

If your tires are deflating more whenever you drive, you are actually taking more money from your pockets.

Why? Simply because the less efficient your tires are, the more gasoline you use, and not just because they deteriorate faster.

It is best to always keep your tires well inflated according to the manufacturer's instructions. Keep in mind that a tire that has been inflated by 2 PSI can actually boost your car's gas use by 1%.

6. Organize your shopping trips

Getting things organized not only makes life easier to bear but can also save more on your expenses.

Consider this: try to budget your food consumption for the week and have all your groceries bought on a single day. It would be best if you can find all of the things you need in a single store. In this way, you can cut back on fuel use.

7. Reduce wind resistance

If you will be driving on a highway, it is best to keep your windows closed so as to lessen that drag. Dragging can aggravate fuel consumption. Remember your physics? It will definitely take more force just to push your car through the wind and this would mean using more gas than usual.

All of these things can, in some way or another, help you save on gas. Just try to be conscious of where your money goes and it will be easier for you to find cost-effective ways to save more money.

**How to save on car repairs**

Tips on How to Save on Car Repairs: The Car Owner's Ultimate Guide Book to Savings

Are you one of those few people who are having trouble in getting their cars repaired and drain their finances as well? If you are, then it is high time you start looking for ways to save on car repairs and save more in your piggy bank.

Defective cars aren't even worthy to be sold without getting all the necessary repairs. You can't even exchange it with another car without getting it repaired.

You are left with no choice at all but to get it fixed. The only problem is that without the appropriate guidelines you need in choosing the right repairs, you can be spending more than what you can afford.

With the high prices going on in the market today, no one can really afford to have their cars repaired in very expensive packages. So you have to think of ways to save more on car repairs.

You can trim down on car repairs and save more cash on an ordinary basis without opting to excessive ways. Here's how you can save on car repairs:

1. Do your homework

One of the greatest problems most motorists encounter is that they spend more on car repairs simply because they didn't choose the best mechanic or repair service for their cars.

Through research, you can identify the right mechanic and the right shop.

2. Take note of the things that need to be repaired

Before you go to your mechanic, it is best to have all the necessary repairs listed on a piece of paper. In this way, you can tell your mechanic right way the things that need to be repaired. This will prevent unnecessary repairs or misunderstandings on the type of repairs that your car needs. Unnecessary repairs will only add up to your repair expenses.

3. Shop and compare

To get the best quotes on car repairs, try to shop around and compare prices. In this way, you can evaluate and compare prices enabling you to find the best quotes possible.

Never grab the first repair shop you find. By looking around, you can still find better shops than what you have right now.

4. Try to make every transaction in black and white

This means that before you commit yourself in a particular repair job, it is best to have the estimate written on a piece of paper. Try to acquire a copy of your own. This will prevent unnecessary accumulation of extra charges, which weren't included on the first estimation.

Keep in mind that not all job repairs were created equal and not all mechanics are honest. So it is best to protect yourself as always.

5. Acquire your car's old parts before you let the mechanic start the repair process

There are certain car parts that can still be rebuilt. So never let your mechanic take the chance of acquiring these things. You can have them repaired on some machine shops and cut back your expenses on the next repair.

6. Know your way around

If you don't know your way around car repairs, it is best to ask someone (definitely not your mechanic) for some second opinions. In this way, you can decide which things need greater considerations.

Besides, if you will just let your mechanic decide on your car's repair process, you might pay more than what you can imagine.

Better yet, read some easy-to-read manuals on car maintenance. In this way, you will learn some important matters regarding car parts. This will enable you to differentiate the important repairs from those that you can do by yourself.

## 7. Ask for the warranty

Some repair shops offer warranties on the services that they make. Take note of this so that you can be sure not to spend another hundred dollars for the same repair in just a few days.

Furthermore, warranties can guarantee high quality repairs so you can be sure that your car and your pocket are in good hands.

Indeed, car repairs can't be avoided. These are the things that you have to learn to live with.

Finding good repair shops aren't that hard. Just try to remember these pointers and you will surely spend less with car repairs.

Also, think about learning how to do the simple chores yourself. That's where those manuals may come in handy. With just a little bit of knowledge you can handle minor maintenance like oil changes, tune-ups, changing windshield wipers and other simple tasks. Learning to do these yourself will result in great savings!

# How to save on home improvement

Cool Tips on How to Save on Home Improvement

Have you ever thought of changing your room's design? Do you think your porch needs a little makeover? Then it is time for you to make some improvements in your home and create a difference.

Home improvement can add sparkle to a dull wall color, a new shade to a dreary interior design, or vigor to a lifeless porch. It simply pertains to the method of refurbishing or repairing a home.

In most cases, an expert executes home improvements. However, with the cost of commodities nowadays, plus the real service fees of "professional handyman," many people have opted to work on their home improvements through their own initiative.

No wonder why the so-called "do-it-yourself" jobs have been pretty popular. Through this process, homeowners can enjoy renovating their own homes like professionals. There are shops that provide seminars or workshops regarding their products and the way homeowners can operate them at home.

There are many types of home improvements. Each category can provide optimum modernization to one's home.

However, home improvement package prices may vary. It is best to identify the right measures to save more on home improvements.

Here are some ways on how to cut back on your home improvement costs:

1. Do your research

Before you start on your home improvement project, it is best to do some extensive research. Try to find out the current prices of home improvement packages available on the market today. It is also best to identify the different factors that can affect the conditions of each type of home improvements.

2. Scout for the best quotes

If you will be hiring a professional, it is best to look for the best price quotes on home improvements. In this way, you will be able to anticipate the possible rates and charges, which will enable you to prepare the required amount. Get quotes from more than one tradesman.

3. Do the math

Before you start buying things that you need for your home improvement, it is best to have everything estimated.

Should you decide to seek the services of a professional you will know how much it will take you to improve your home. You can't easily be fooled by anyone because you know exactly the cost of expenses.

Besides, having a rough estimate of your home improvement plans will enable you to control your expenses. You can focus on the areas that need to be prioritized. Once you have set a specific budget on it, you can now consider the other areas without having to spend more than what you can afford.

4. Decide whether you can do it yourself or you should hire a

professional

If you want to save more on your home improvements, it is best to decide if you can do the project yourself or you really need to hire a professional.

It is unwise to assume that you can do the job just to trim down your expenses, where in fact, you don't have the slightest idea how to start the job.

Insisting to do the job yourself will only end up in waste or destruction. It is best to hire a professional if you really want to save on your home improvement.

5. Ask for recommendations

Word of mouth is considered as one of the best advertising strategy in marketing. It is also one of the best ways to ask for some help about the things that you are not familiar with.

For example, if you don't have any idea about home improvements, it is best to ask your friends, relatives, or even colleagues about home improvements.

They can give you some pointers about home improvements based on their own experience. Tried and tested, their idea about home improvements can really help you make a difference.

6. Find the best contractor

If you wish to save on home improvements through contractors, it is best to hire the best. You can do this by checking on your contractor's capabilities and certifications. In this way, you can be sure that the services you pay are reliable and efficient.

Try to keep these things in mind to save on your home improvement projects. Keep in mind that home improvements need not be expensive. You can beautify your home without having to go overboard.

**How to save on home heating and energy**

How to Save on Home Heating Energy: Superb Saving Ideas

To say that you can save on your home's heating system and energy isn't an understatement. Reduced bills on your electricity, maximized heating system, and a whole lot of energy saving phenomenon are things you don't see everyday but desire to obtain.

Everybody longs to reduce his or her expenses on energy and heating systems. People don't work just to pay the utility bills alone.

The greatest reason for this dilemma is the on-going increase of energy consumption charges. Everything seems to have high prices nowadays. It is best to trim down the other expenses in which you have control of, such as energy consumption.

One of the best examples of energy use are home heating systems. However, heaters can eat up bigger portions in your electricity bill. In fact, statistical reports prove that heaters are one of the largest energy consumers in every home, that is, more than half of the consumption rate in a given year.

For this reason, it is imperative to think of ways to save on heating systems so as to save on energy consumption as well. As you save on these items, you get more value for your money.

But how? Things are, most of the time, easier said than done. So if you think that it is easy to maximize your heaters and save more on energy, think again.

To help you, here is a list of some energy saving tips that will help you cut back on your furnaces' energy consumption.

1. Use solar energy

Natural is always the best. To save more on energy, it is best to use solar energy when using water heaters in your home's heating system. In this way, you trap natural heat coming from the sun. You will consume less energy.

With the solar energy utilized in your home's heating system, you can start heating your water for showers or revolutionize your home's heating system and still reduce your electricity bill.

2. Inspect your home

To maximize your home's heating system, it is best to inspect your house for any leakage. Leaks will let the heat seep out from your home, thus, absorbing cold from the outside. Most of the areas that leakage starts to develop are in the windows, doors, and fireplaces.

Once identified, it is best to take some proper actions as soon as possible so as to cut back any unnecessary costs on energy.

3. Use heaters on frequently used rooms only

To save more energy, only use heaters on areas that are frequently visited and used by your household. For rooms that are not being used, try to turn off the thermostat or close the windows to utilize natural heat.

Close the vents to the rooms that you are not using.

By doing so, you can cut back your energy consumption through your furnace by as much as 50%.

4. Insulate

One of the biggest secrets in maximizing your home's heating system is insulation. A properly and well insulated home can guarantee a comfortable home without using too much energy. Thus, you can save more money by cutting back your energy consumption.

It is best to use some insulating devices on your roof, windows, and other areas that need padding. This will block the heat in and keep it from escaping the house.

5. Get a good heating system

Of course, you can never guarantee lower energy bill if not for an efficient heating system. A defective heating system can use twice as much energy as one that is functioning properly. The tendency is to use more force just to boost more heat, and the more force the heating device use, the more energy it will consume.

Besides, defective products would require frequent visits to repair shops and that would be additional expenses for you.

All of these things can help you maximize your heating system and save more energy. In this way, you can save more money and use it on other things that need prioritization.

Depending on where you live, consider switching from electric to gas or vice versa. Electricity is less costly in some areas while in other areas gas is the better choice. Do your research for the area you live in and determine which better meets your needs.

**How to save on phone service**

How to Save on Phone Service

Since its inception, long distance calls have created a niche in the telecommunications industry in the United States. In fact, reports from the Federal Communications Commission have attested that more than 1.75% of consumers' general expenses are attributed to phone services such as long distance calls.

No wonder why many Americans are squanderers when it comes to phone services. In 1992, reports show that the average amount that the Americans spend on long distance calls amount to $10.3 billion.

Now, the question lies on whether these expenses are

maintained and paid by the phone companies' subscribers. Come to think of it, the utilization of phone services has increased to a level where consumers can no longer pay their dues.

What happens next is that some phone companies were required to make some cutbacks on their operating expenses.

But to some, cutbacks aren't the ultimate solution. Most of the phone companies have come up with revolutionary added features that are more functional and multidimensional. These items seek to entice people to subscribe to phone services once more and gain back the popularity that the phone companies used to have.

With these phone companies have created different choices for long distance calls. Each feature is designed to suit the needs of every customer or subscriber.

The usual phone service options are the bundled, traditional, VoIP, wireless, and calling cards. Each service has its own pros and cons, but all of them were catered to provide optimum phone services to their subscribers.

Sounds good enough? Think again.

With the high prices of commodities nowadays, it pays a lot to save on your phone services and earn that extra money you will need in the near future.

But how?

First, keep in mind that not all phone services were created equal. And even if they may vary according to their rates and charges, consumers can find ways on how to save on phone services, regardless of their classification and the type of service that they provide.

Here are some few good tips:

1. Select a good plan

To save more on your phone services, it is best to choose a good plan first. You can do this by checking on the phone companies available on the market today. Compare their rates and choose the best plan.

However, experts say that it would be better if you choose from the three leading phone companies in the industry. Statistical reports show that you can save by as much as 50% or more as compared to other phone companies.

2. Identify your "calling pattern"

Try to identify your calling pattern based on the latest three bills. Analyze the flow of calls and pinpoint those that create particular patterns.

Once you have identified them, you can easily detect which areas you call frequently, at what time, and for how long.

So if you have clearly identified your calling pattern," it will be easier for you to save more on your bills.

3. Flexibility

Choose a phone service that gives you the flexibility to adapt to your needs. This will guarantee optimum communication service because you can alter or modify any feature that will correspond to your needs.

For example, if you have been previously subscribed to a post-paid long distance phone service and you wish to convert your phone service into prepaid, it is best to choose a long distance carrier that will allow you to do such thing without the extra charges.

In this way, you can save on the service fees (for the conversion) as well as on the long distance charges. With prepaid, you can now control your long distance activities.

4. Be wary on the promotions

Not all freebies and promotions can be good for you. There are some promotions that may only lure to try a particular phone service, only to find out that you get double charges in return after the promotion is over.

With this, you not only passed the chance of saving more money on your phone services, but you also missed the chance to enjoy real savings without having to spend more than what you can afford.

Indeed, saving on phone services can trim down your expenses in a month. It is best to remember these pointers very well as they may come in handy sometime in the future.

## How to save on major appliances

Your Guide to Saving on Major Appliances

Saving is one of the most important things to consider in budgeting. Whether you are a parent of two or three or a student or an independent planning to move to a different place, saving should always be put as a number one priority.

For example, moving into a new area requires basic household appliances such as fridge, washing machine, stove, and heater. Normally, these appliances would cost you thousands of dollars if one would not consider some of the cost-effective tips in buying major appliances.

With that being said, below are just some of the cost-effective and saving tips in purchasing new appliances for your new abode.

a. Evaluate your Wants and Needs. Appliances will always be part of our daily lives but with a starter, one would have to evaluate and think about the most important household appliances to buy.

First, think about the things that you should need when moving to a new house. Would you prefer buying a fridge in favor of a new sofa or a convenient ice-making machine against a reasonable fridge?

While these add-ons are important, this should also require a lot of thinking in order to keep all those that are important and set aside those that will provide luxury. Worth mentioning is the amount of electricity that one has to consume when using these add-on products.

b. Size – accommodating your newly purchased electrical appliances can be fun if you have enough or available space. It isn't wise to purchase a huge refrigerator when you only have few square inches of space available for your immediate kitchen needs.

For families, parents should also take into consideration the type of appliances, which will be able to supply all the needs for the family.

A 5.0-kilogram washer would definitely not suffice in a family of 5. In such cases, one would have to consider purchasing those that are of heavy-duty type of major appliances.

You will save more on buying in bulk than for one that won't accommodate most of the clothing used for a week by a single person alone.

c. Consult with Comparison Shops. The 1999 Consumer Literacy Consortium report provides enough reason for consumers to compare price around before they do the actual purchasing on major appliances.

Basically, for people who are determined to make the purchase, they would usually shop on a single appliance center and don't bother to shop around and compare prices at nearby stores.

The consumer report provided information about the benefits of comparing prices on the market before doing the actual buying and the importance of shopping online for auctions and sales.

More often than not, leveraging on secondhand appliances is better than procuring a new one specially when one would look into similar features and durability standard. This intelligent buying will save you hundreds of dollars as expected and allot savings to other home stuffs that in turn provides additional luxury in your part.

d. Annual Buying Guide – Local libraries today keep some records of buying guides and ratings and prices on some of the major appliances nationwide. These buying guides and consumer literacy reports provide exclusive and substantial information on performance (durability), price, and quality among other things.

The report also maintains a database where you can compare prices from coast to coast and details on handling and packaging of merchandises should one would interest on buying them.

e. Where to Buy – Sometimes, it isn't about the name of the merchandiser that matters when filling your home with major appliances. It's about how you would search the local market and the net to find shopping exclusives and sales of appliance items whose features and performance match specifically to the needs and wants of your family.

These buying techniques won't only free you on your budget but provide you additional leverage on saving for future appliance needs.

f.     Negotiate – In almost every part of the selling process, negotiation takes place when you would interest on purchasing the item after making a careful review of its features. Getting the best bet lies in your ability to making compromises.

Most stores would drop prices when needed and when the customer asks for it and when one is purchasing refurbished items.

## How to save on furniture

Tips On How To Save On Purchasing Your Furniture

Saving money on purchasing your furniture for your home doesn't necessarily mean sacrificing the quality of the product. Of course, you want only the best worth for your very own home. The following are keys and tips that you can follow to save an awful lot of money when you procure your dream furniture:

1. Look for Furniture on SALE!

More often than not, the best deal on Furniture on Sale comes every January and July. And if you're looking for outdoor furniture, August is the best time ever! Also, most of the furniture companies have their furniture set on very low prices every end of the month for sole purpose of their clearance.

Majority of the retail furniture companies function on monthly basis, computing their sales, releasing their promotions and introducing new furniture.

This means that at the end of the month, there will be certain pieces of furniture that won't be offered the following month, thus these lines of products will be offered at a very low price. Another reason will be because most of the furniture companies hire sales people and pay them by commission.

These people will definitely have their own bills to pay so would be a little more desperate to make the sale, hence, could be giving a better deal for your most wanted furniture. You can definitely take advantage of their eagerness.

2. Visit your Favorite Furniture Stores

Check all the possible Furniture Shops first and find the best deal before finally purchasing your piece. Most regional and national furniture retailers have outlet shops where suspended, distressed and returned merchandise is being sold at low prices.

Form a habit of checking these shops frequently —you never know when the right furniture is going to be waiting for you at its best deal!

3. Apply for the Credit Card being offered by the Furniture Shop

Some wholesale furniture shops offer in-store credit cards. These credit cards normally give you the best discounts on the furniture inside that furniture center. All you have to do is apply for this credit card and you can get discounts for your desired piece of fixture.

Then, you may pay for your credit card bill the following day using the money that you have allotted for the furniture; this will save you the finance charge that the credit card company may cost you.

## 4. Search the World Wide Web

After seeing a certain piece of furniture either at the store near you or in a certain magazine, check the Net for this certain product. Just enter the manufacturer's name and if that piece has its name as well. Use the famous search engines like Google and Yahoo.

There are some Online Shops that may offer your certain furniture at a very good discount. However, it is imperative to check the shipping rates and taxes that may be applied with the product. Please don't just rely on the price that is posted on the initial site for it may mislead you on possible additional charges.

## 5. Go Directly To The Manufacturer

If you live within a few miles of a furniture manufacturer, it is strongly suggested that you visit their shops for you may get the lowest possible price for your preferred furniture.

## 6. Buy Used Furniture

One of the best ways of saving your hard-earned money is by going to Second Hand shops for certain furniture. You may opt to have your fixture reupholstered or refinished by your favorite carpenter to put the touch of your individuality and giving it the smell of novelty.

More often than not, the total price of your furniture plus the cost of the repair is still a lot cheaper than buying a totally new piece. Stores selling used furniture are almost everywhere especially in major cities.

**How to save on clothing**

Saving Guide on Clothing

Clothes can be really costly, especially when all the fads and trends come and go as the seasons. It is very possible to save money when buying your clothes. You just need to have the strategies and tactics on how you can save your money. Here are some tips on how to save when buying your clothes:

Don't buy in Season clothes – different line of clothes come every season. And more often than not, they normally release new clothes at very high prices and normally they go down after a few months. Key is just patience to wait.

For example, when winter comes, coats and sweaters are released, however, after a month, normal Sale or bargain prices will now be tagged on these clothes. If you were smart enough to wait, you can still wear these clothes during the remaining days of winter and the coming fall.

- Wait for Factory Sales – when Factories put out their sale season, clothes can be cut from 40%-90% off the original price. Imagine how big this saving is! Also, going directly to the Manufacturer's store is a helpful tip on getting a good deal on clothes.

- Garage Sales – these are very popular stores and places where you can get your clothes at really, really low prices. Find garage sales that are put up by families, in this way, chances of getting quality clothes are much higher than those garage sales that have been put up for commercial purposes already.

However, it is important to remember and avoid buying clothes just because the prices are really low, you might not even wear the clothes, and the concept of saving is put to waste.

- Bargain – always visit your favorite store and befriend the sales people there. You can then ask for the possible dates of SALE and bargain wherein you can save at a minimum of 20% off the original price of your desired clothes.

- Buy two different sizes and two different colors – If you have kids, it is very advisable to actually get two sizes, since children grow up really fast. Also, buying two colors to have variety, only if the clothes are already at their reduced rates.

- Shop Online – nowadays, there are many clothing stores online. And, most of the clothing lines have their own websites where you can online shop.

Like the regular stores, the online shops have their season for SALE and BARGAINS as well. Just make a habit of checking regularly your favorite clothing line to wait for these awaited bargains.

- Sign up for your Favorite Boutique's mailing list – be sure to sign up for your favorite clothing store's mailing list, newsletter and catalogs. In this way, you will be updated and be the first one to know of the upcoming On Sale Items and the new releases of the trendy clothes as well.

- Coupon Codes and Coupon Cards – if shopping online is your thing, there are many coupon codes that can be found online that could give you a cut off of the original price of your favorite online store. Some of the coupon code sites are the www.couponcabin.com and www.keycode.com.

All you have to do is look for the "apparel" category code and you will be given your choices of retailers. You can also put the "online coupon" or "coupon code" in your favorite search engines such as Google and you will be given a list of sites that could provide you best deals for your retailers.

- In-Store Credit Cards – many boutiques nowadays, offer in-store credit cards. All you need to do is apply for a credit card of your own, especially if you have a favorite store where you frequently buy your clothes. Normally, these credit cards give good discounts on clothes being sold in that particular boutique.

Also, the cardholders normally get special coupons, birthday discounts and other relative discounts every holiday and often you can get a minimum of 5% up to 15% discounts.

Another benefit of these is free shipping, being updated of the new arrival of clothes and rebates. However, this tactic only is beneficial if you plan to pay your credit card bill a day after you have purchased the product. This is because credit card companies charge an awful lot of finance fees and interests. It may not even counterbalance the savings you intentionally wanted in applying for the credit card.

- Get a part-time job at your favorite store – a lot of shoppers apply and get part time jobs on their favorite boutique. This will give them extra money for their job and employee's discounts on the clothes being sold in that particular store.

**How to save on groceries**

Save Money on Your Grocery Shopping

One of the basic necessities is your stock of groceries. And your budget for the groceries could make or break your budget for your weekly funds that should be allotted on other things. This is how flexible the budget for the groceries could be. This flexibility should be handled properly.

Here are tips on how you can save money for your groceries:

- Make sure you aren't hungry before you go to the Grocery Store – studies have shown that shoppers tend to buy more in the grocery stores when they are hungry. This is the reason why some grocery shops have their bakery along the entrance of the store.

The smell of the freshly baked breads and cakes could really make you hungry. And this could make you shop and spend more than what you intended.

The best way to handle this is to make sure your stomach is not empty, if no food can be taken; drink at least a glass or two of water. Shopping when you're full will help you combat the temptations of the

mouth-watering smells inside the grocery store.

- Try to look up and down on the shelves – make sure that you search the higher and lower shelves. The more expensive brands are normally located on the shelves on your chest level. The cheaper or generic brands are either located below or higher than your average sight.

- Shop alone – try to find time to go to the grocery store by yourself. When you ask for helpers, they tend to increase your bill.

- Go to the store at the early time of the day – when you go to the grocery store early in the morning, you tend to finish with your list a little faster, thus avoiding the need to roam around and get attracted to unnecessary expenses.

- Shop when you are in a good mood – when you shop and you feel tired, you tend to buy more sweets, chocolates and high-carbohydrates. And when you are mad, you tend to buy more junk food.

- Don't buy non-grocery items – grocery stores normally sell some non-grocery items like contact lens and painkillers. These products normally cost more at the grocery stores.

- Always bring your calculator – make sure to shop with your calculator. In this way, you can easily compute how much you save when buying in-packs or individually wrapped items.

- Check your receipts after shopping, mistakes can happen no matter how much you avoid them. Remember that every cent counts.

Buy foods that are fresh, cheap and seasoned. With fewer dealers involved, the cheaper, fresher and better quality of food that you can get for your family.

Make sure to double-check the weights of the pre-packed goodies that you buy. Sometimes they lack a little pound or weigh less than what they normally should. Make it a point that you get all your hard-earned money's worth.

When you specifically went to your favorite grocery shop for a definite item on sale and suddenly knowing that it's no longer available. Make sure that you make a rain check and ask for the next stocks to arrive. So that you'll be early the next time the stocks reach the store.

- Check the ends and edges of the grocery store. More often than not, the healthy and fresher foods are located at the ends of the grocery shops. Fruits, vegetables, Dairy products and meats are examples of these.

Avoid walking thru the main areas, since these regions are normally where the products are very expensive and cost more.

It's important to focus on the price of the item. Make sure to check the other brands to be certain of getting the best deal. Also, buy only what you need. Sometimes, you get deceived when you get to buy things that are on sale even if you don't need them. If this happens, you didn't get the bargain no matter how cheap it seemed.

Don't be misled with the brilliant colored packaging of the grocery shops. They normally pack certain items simply to attract. Focus on your list and buy things that you need.

# How to save on vacations

Save on your Vacations

It is true that after all saving and cutting down all the expenses from other things like clothes, appliances and groceries, you and your family deserves a well planned vacation at least once a year.

However, it is still imperative to save as much as you can while having your vacation. Especially, while you are on vacation, more often than not, the budget is a tough thing to keep.

Here are the ways on how you can save on your vacations:

Save on Airfares – Make arrangements and book your flights ahead of time. Airlines normally have promos if you purchase your tickets in advance. Also, Airline tickets sell evening flights a little cheaper than those of the day flights.

If you are purchasing your Airline tickets from the travel agencies in your area, make sure to scout for the best deal for ticket prices. When buying tickets for your family or for four or more passengers, there will be special discounts, be sure to ask for these opportunities to save.

- If possible, plan your vacation during the off-peak seasons. The travel agency has its peak and off-peak seasons. Make sure to research these dates. Every destination has its own determination of peak seasons. Airfares and hotel accommodation are much cheaper during the lean seasons.

Make sure to bring packaged snacks that are purchased at supermarkets. Eating and dining out in restaurants can be really expensive especially if you are traveling in groups.

For road/land trips, as much as possible, bring your own car for your tour. Car rentals can be really expensive and unnecessary. Don't forget an auto-check up from your favorite and trusted mechanic before leaving for vacation.

Don't forget to fill your gas tank. This will allow you to shop for cheap gasoline stations and avoid unplanned stops along the way.

Don't pay for your vacation in credit unless you are very certain that you can pay on time. Interests on such credit can be a burden especially after having fun on your vacation.

Don't forget to turn off ongoing expenses while you're away on vacation. Discontinue your newspaper deliveries. Temporarily cancel your internet service when on vacation for more than a month. Turn off your gas and electric heater when you are away from home.

- Planning in advance can help you save with your budget. Prepare proper clothes to bring for the destination. Buying emergency clothes for cold climate can be really costly and should be avoided since you can pack all these from home. In this way, you can spend your vacation money on other important things.

Always keep your receipts and track your records for all the expenses during the vacation. These can help for future vacations and can also be deductibles for taxes if you are on business trips.

- Plan for your Accommodation – considering homes of relatives or close friends can help you save on your vacation. You can also choose paid accommodations with cooking facilities. This can help you save money from eating out at restaurants. Take advantage of

special offers from hotels or motels offering "family" rates.

Be sure to take advantage of free tourist attractions such as parks, museums, free gardens and monuments.

- Consider an adventure trip or "camping" vacation. This is really cheap and fun. Some national parks and forest campgrounds only charge you minimal fee for your stay, and some even let you rent your tents. The idea of marshmallows with hotdogs on your bonfire can be really exiting.

Don't forget to budget your money for your souvenir allowance. Don't buy unnecessary souvenir items that can only be sold at your garage sale the following year. Buy something useful.

Be sure to have portable irons when traveling. Press jobs at the hotels are really expensive.

Don't forget to bring your first aid kit that should contain, medicines, alcohol, and stuffs that can heal minor bruises and cuts.

- Leave and entrust your pets to your friends or families

instead of bringing them along.

## How to save on prescription drugs

Save on your Prescription Drugs

There are many money-saving tips in purchasing prescription drugs and one way to doing this is to go through all your resources and look into other possibilities which will help you accomplish the task on saving.

A recent national study on prescription drugs show that most Americans are using more prescription drugs at a younger age. Oftentimes, people resorted to ineffective medical products in favor of more potent yet approved products by the government.

The study revealed that the Americans spending have increased to twenty five percent annually between 1996 and 1999.

The same thing applies to seniors. It shows that more than fifty percent of the senior citizens aren't covered by any insurance inclusive of medicine benefits specifically for prescription drugs.

The following tips provides the best recommendations for saving on prescription drugs and how one would be able to manage to keep them fresh and save on future need of such drugs.

a) Go for Generics - Don't forget to request the generic brand of the drug prescribed to you. Up to fifty percent or more can be saved from the cost of the initially prescribed medicine by your doctors.

Using the generic brand of medicine can help you save on the average cost of each medicine. Most pharmacies don't offer generic brands unless specifically asked.

b) Make Comparisons - Make sure to compare the prices from different pharmacies before finally purchasing. Values can really vary. Some pharmacies can offer certain discounts on specific brands of medicines.

c) Look for Discounts - Members of AARP can receive discounts especially from mail-order pharmacy discounts. Check the Veterans Administration to check if you are eligible for some veterans' benefits.

d) Keep Drugs Away from Sunlight. Make sure to store your medicines and pills away from moisture and heat to ensure the optimal potency of these drugs. Most drugs, when exposed to sunlight, tend to lose their potency.

This happens because the very chemical nature of the drug is destroyed and thereby losing its original chemical effect on the body.

e) Talk to your Doctor - It is definitely okay to ask and inquire to your doctors about the medicines prescribed to you. You are still in control of your own health. And most doctors even expect you to ask for less expensive brands of the medicines written on your prescriptions.

You are the only one responsible for your health; it is necessary that you are well informed of all the medicines and medications you are taking.

f) Assess yourself - It is imperative to keeping a daily "record" of your physical health. It is really easy to research on your medical condition over the Internet. Maximize your resources.

Comply with the treatment plan that you and your physician have designed for your health. Carefully and specifically following this plan can help you save money and avoid future recurrence of the existing illness.

g) Double it Up - The fastest way to saving money is by dividing the drug cost in half. One way to do this is through literally cutting a drug in half to attain the exact dosage desired.

For example, if your doctor prescribed you a 40 mg dosage, you can buy the 80 mg tablet and just split it in half. This is since there is a very minimal difference on the price of the 40 mg to the 80 mg. You can save by doing this technique.

h) Ask for the samples. A lot of pharmaceutical companies supply their pharmacies with more than enough of sample medicines. They are very eager to let people try their products.

All you have to do is ask your pharmacists. This can be really safe for short-term illnesses, and could help you save money before buying.

i) Know what your medical insurance covers. Make sure that you fully understand its coverage before signing up with the plan. Be specific of the maximum amount of your co-payments will pay for the whole year. More often than not, a health plan only approves for certain pre-approved drugs.

Don't forget to consult your family doctor before completely signing up for the plan. Open formularies present more drugs but cost of the plan will definitely vary.

j) It costs less to buy your medicine in bulk. However, make sure to discuss this with your physician, some medicines aren't advisable to be purchased in bulk.

www.ingramcontent.com/pod-product-compliance
Lightning Source LLC
Chambersburg PA
CBHW020614220526
45463CB00006B/2586